BEHIND THE SCENES
HOCKEY

by James Monson

Lerner Publications ◆ Minneapolis

Lerner Publications Company
A division of Lerner Publishing Group, Inc.
241 First Avenue North
Minneapolis, MN 55401 USA

For reading levels and more information, look up this title at www.lernerbooks.com.

The images in this book are used with the permission of: © John Russell/NHLI/National Hockey League/Getty Images, p. 1; David Becker/NHLI/National Hockey League/Getty Images, pp. 4–5; © Ethan Miller/Getty Images Sport/Getty Images, p. 6; © Dardalnna/Shutterstock.com, pp. 8–9; © Jill Brady/Portland Press Herald/Getty Images, pp. 10–11; © Andy Marlin/NWHL/National Hockey League/Getty Images, p. 13; © Len Redkoles/NHLI/National Hockey League/Getty Images, p. 16; © Peter Kneffel/picture alliance/Getty Images, p. 18; © Eliot J. Schechter/NHLI/National Hockey League/Getty Images, pp. 14–15; © Robin Alam/Icon Sportswire/Getty Images, p. 19; © Pat Greenhouse/The Boston Globe/Getty Images, pp. 20–21; © Richard Lautens/Toronto Star/Getty Images, pp. 22–23; © Andre Ringuette/NHLI/National Hockey League/Getty Images, pp. 24–25; © Abbie Parr/Tie Break Tens/Getty Images Sport/Getty Images, p. 26; © Jody Dingle/Shutterstock.com, pp. 28–29.

Front cover: © John Russell/NHLI/National Hockey League/Getty Images.

Main body text set in Myriad Pro.
Typeface provided by Adobe.

Library of Congress Cataloging-in-Publication Data

Names: Monson, James, 1994– author.
Title: Behind the scenes hockey / James Monson.
Description: Minneapolis : Lerner Publications, [2020] | Series: Inside the sport | Includes bibliographical references and index. | Audience: Age 7–11. | Audience: Grade 4 to 6.
Identifiers: LCCN 2018047661 (print) | LCCN 2018053981 (ebook) | ISBN 9781541556300 (eb pdf) | ISBN 9781541556041 (lb : alk. paper) | ISBN 9781541574380 (pb)
Subjects: LCSH: Hockey—Training—Juvenile literature. | Hockey players—Health and hygiene—Juvenile literature. | Hockey players—Conduct of life—Juvenile literature. | Hockey players—Charitable contributions—Juvenile literature. | National Hockey League—Juvenile literature.
Classification: LCC GV847.25 (ebook) | LCC GV847.25 .M66 2020 (print) | DDC 796.962—dc23

LC record available at https://lccn.loc.gov/2018047661

Manufactured in the United States of America
1-CG-7/15/19

CONTENTS

GETTING THAT FIRST STANLEY CUP

When Alexander Ovechkin and the Washington Capitals made it to the National Hockey League (NHL) championship series in 2018, they faced a tough opponent in the Vegas Golden Knights. Ovechkin had played with the Capitals for more than twelve years. He would do anything to help his team win this best-of-seven series and take home the Stanley Cup.

Las Vegas won Game 1 at home. But the Capitals stormed back to win the next three games. At Game 5, Washington was just one win

Alexander Ovechkin holds the Stanley Cup above his head after he and the Capitals won Game 5 of the 2018 NHL championship series. ▶

FACTS
at a Glance

- Pro hockey players are on the ice for about one minute at a time during games.

- Hockey players are eligible to be drafted by NHL teams when they are eighteen years old.

- Women must finish their junior season of college hockey before they are eligible to be drafted by National Women's Hockey League (NWHL) teams.

- The NHL has been around for more than one hundred years. The National Women's Hockey League (NWHL) began in 2015.

- Off the ice, professional hockey players work out to stay in shape.

- Many professional hockey players participate in charity work.

Capitals players celebrate winning the Stanley Cup.

away from the championship. The Golden Knights were hoping to keep their season alive. Ovechkin had other ideas. He got the puck on his stick in the second period. He fired a shot into the back of the net. Goal! That helped Washington take a 2–1 lead.

The game came down to the final few minutes. Ovechkin was giving his all to help the Capitals win. He fell to the ice to block any Vegas shot he could with his body. With less than a second remaining, the Golden Knights won a faceoff near the Washington goal. Vegas forward Erik Haula fired a shot to the net. But Washington defender Brooks Orpik stopped the puck. The clock read 0:00. The game was over. The Capitals were the 2018 Stanley Cup champions!

Ovechkin skated to his team's goal to celebrate. He soon held the trophy over his head proudly. He had worked hard to get to that championship moment. There is so much more to being a successful hockey player than what happens on the ice. Hard work behind the scenes makes a difference.

CHAPTER 1

CLIMBING THE RANKS

Most professional hockey players start at an early age. Organized youth hockey leagues often begin when players are five or six years old. These young players work on skating. They also practice basic hockey skills such as holding the stick and shooting the puck.

Youth hockey leagues get more competitive as the players get older. Players start traveling to other cities for games and tournaments at about ten years old. Some teams travel long distances.

Skating is an essential skill for hockey players. It is one of many basic skills players learn at a young age. ▶

High school hockey players dream of one day being in the NHL, NWHL, or competing in the Olympic Games with the US national teams. ▶

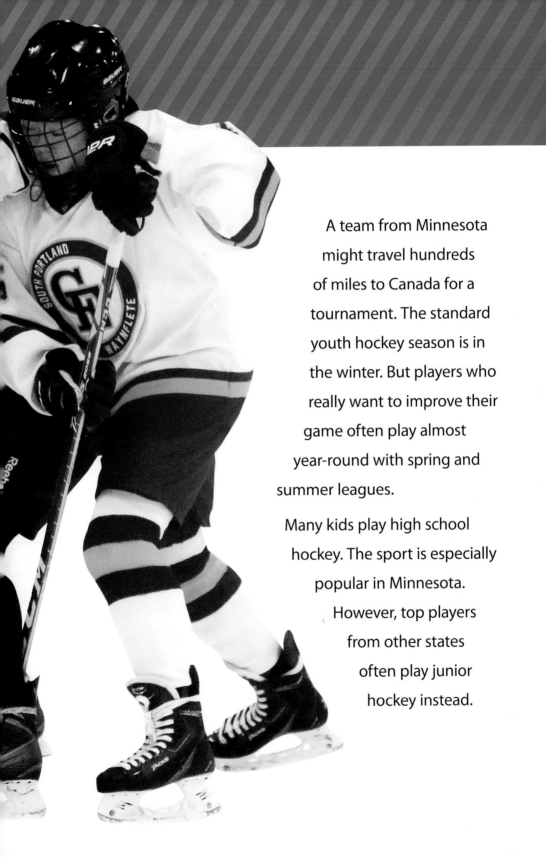

A team from Minnesota might travel hundreds of miles to Canada for a tournament. The standard youth hockey season is in the winter. But players who really want to improve their game often play almost year-round with spring and summer leagues.

Many kids play high school hockey. The sport is especially popular in Minnesota. However, top players from other states often play junior hockey instead.

Those leagues are for players aged sixteen to twenty. They are often more competitive than local high school leagues. Players might have to move away from home to play junior hockey. After high school, some top players move on to college hockey teams. Others stay with their junior teams.

When players turn eighteen, they are eligible for the NHL Draft. When a player is selected by an NHL team, he can choose to continue playing at the college or junior level. Some top players go straight to the NHL. Auston Matthews of the Toronto Maple Leafs did that in 2016.

Women can also play college hockey after high school. If they are good enough, they may also play with the US national team. They do this outside of the college

Hilary Knight of the Boston Pride takes a shot at goalie Brianna McLaughlin of the Buffalo Beauts.

hockey season. The top players continue playing with Team USA after college. They also might play professionally in the NWHL. Players cannot be drafted by an NWHL team until after their junior year of college. They cannot play in the NWHL until they have played four years in college.

CHAPTER 2

A DAY IN THE LIFE

On game day, most professional hockey players plan their schedules ahead of time. This allows them to stay focused on the game. The plan starts in the morning with breakfast. Players might eat foods such as fruit or mixed nuts to feel energized. These foods contain vitamins and minerals that can help players get back some of the energy they might have lost during a game or practice.

Florida Panthers players have a morning skate on game day. ▶

Claude Giroux of the
Philadelphia Flyers gets
ready in the locker
room before a game. ▶

Players head to the rink to participate in a morning skate. They work on different plays. Sometimes coaches show players different strategies to use in that night's game. When the morning skate is over, players head back to the locker room. All players change into street clothes. The top players are often interviewed at their lockers by media reporters. Others continue changing and talking with teammates and coaches. Soon it's time for a nap at home or at their hotel. Players feel refreshed when they wake up, and they head back to the arena.

Many players are superstitious about game days. This affects how they get ready for games. Some players put on their equipment the exact same way before each game.

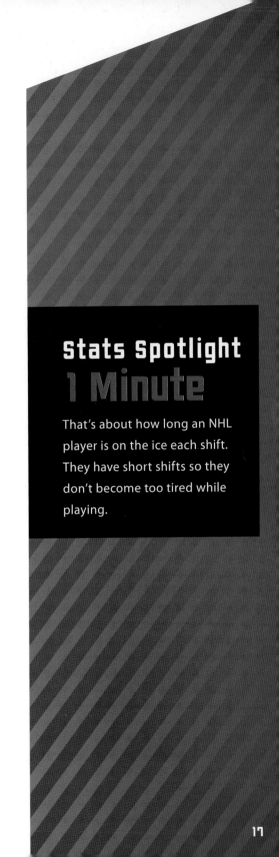

Stats Spotlight
1 Minute

That's about how long an NHL player is on the ice each shift. They have short shifts so they don't become too tired while playing.

US Women's National Team players celebrate a gold-medal win against Canada at the 2018 Winter Olympics in South Korea.

Retired NHL great Wayne Gretzky used to drink beverages in a certain order. He would drink Diet Coke, ice water, Gatorade, and then another Diet Coke.

Once players are ready, they skate around again to warm up. Soon the announcer introduces the starters for the game, and someone performs the national anthem. After that, it's time to drop the puck!

Players skate in short shifts. When they are on the bench, they talk strategy with their coaches and teammates. They're also catching their breath. They drink water or sports drinks.

At the end of the game, the winning team's players skate over to their goalie to celebrate. If it's an important win, there's a lot of hugging and cheering. Players then shake hands with the opposing team.

Then it's back to the locker room. Players shower and eat a postgame snack. Reporters return to the locker room to ask about the game. Reporters may want to talk to the player who scored the game-winning goal. If it's a home game, players head home afterward. If they're on the road, they'll go to a hotel, or they might get straight on a plane for their next stop. Since games usually take place a few days apart, it's soon time to start preparing for the next game.

◄ Nate Schmidt of the Vegas Golden Knights skates during a game.

CHAPTER 3

STAYING ON TOP

Even when not on the ice, hockey players are often still working. They practice their skills. They work to stay healthy and in shape. This training on off days can be just as important as the work right before a game.

Diet is one important thing players think about off the ice. Players often eat lean meats and vegetables. They want to fuel their bodies with healthy food. Some players, including Alexander Ovechkin, prefer grain foods, such as pasta.

Zdeno Chara of the Boston Bruins eats a plant-based diet to stay healthy. ▶

Toronto Maple Leafs players practice in a ▶ summer skate.

Hockey players also have to think about recovering from games. Their bodies take a beating when they play. This can include bruises or strains. There are different ways players try to feel better. They may spend time in hot or cold water. Some players try acupuncture to ease their pain.

During games, players try to be as safe as possible. They use the most advanced equipment, such as special helmet padding that can help prevent concussions. Coaches are also teaching players to be safer when checking one another to cut down on the number of injuries.

When the season ends, players take some time off. But about a month or two before the season begins, players start skating regularly again. The closer players get to the season, the more on-ice work they do. Players who live in the same area during the summer might get together to play informal pick-up games. This allows players to have fun while also practicing and staying in shape.

CHAPTER 4

OFF-ICE IMPRESSIONS

Professional hockey players put time and effort into building relationships with their fans. Many professional athletes give back to their communities. Teams often send their players to hospitals to visit sick patients. Players also participate in charity events. This work helps the athletes become more popular. But more importantly, it helps the community.

Hockey players are also very passionate about getting more people to play the sport. They often help youth teams or teams for people with disabilities.

Blake Coleman of the New Jersey Devils signs autographs for fans. ▶

Members of the US Women's National Team make a public appearance with tennis stars Serena and Venus Williams.

Brock Boeser of the Vancouver Canucks has supported Minnesota Special Hockey, a program for players who have special needs. Olympic gold medalists Jocelyne Lamoureux-Davidson and Monique Lamoureux-Morando have donated thousands of dollars so girls can afford equipment to play hockey.

Outside of helping the community, players might spend time in the off-season traveling around the world. Some appear on TV or at events such as the ESPYs. This helps increase their public image. Many players also interact with fans on social media such as Twitter or Instagram. Hilary Knight of the US Women's National Team posts pictures on Instagram when she travels or when she's hanging out with her teammates.

As the sport of hockey continues to change, players will always be looking for ways to improve. The sport is growing, which means the competition is getting tougher. Players have to keep working on and off the ice so that one day they can become champions.

Stats Spotlight
1.1 Million

This is the number of Twitter followers P. K. Subban of the Nashville Predators has. Subban has become a popular figure by posting about his life off the ice and the charity work he does in Montreal, Canada, where he started his NHL career. Subban has donated millions of dollars to help a children's hospital there. He visits children in the hospital and shares videos from his visits online.

YOUR TURN

Most top players never stop trying to improve their hockey skills. They work on their shooting, skating, and other skills that are needed to be successful at hockey. Young players want to practice many of these same skills.

One way for young players to work on their skating is by playing freeze tag. First, get a group of friends together. Put on skates and hit the ice. One player is "it" at the start of the game. That player chases the others and tries to tag someone. Once a player is tagged, she must freeze until someone who isn't "it" comes by to unfreeze her. This is a great way for players to work on their speed along with starting and stopping quickly on their skates.

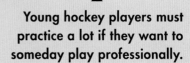

▲
Young hockey players must practice a lot if they want to someday play professionally.

If a player is alone, he can practice speed and stickhandling with a stick, a puck, and a few cones. Use about eight cones and set them in a straight line from one end of the ice to the other. Skate around each cone while using the stick to hold on to the puck. Go down the line of cones and try to keep the puck on the stick the entire time.

GLOSSARY

acupuncture
a way to relieve pain by pushing needles into certain parts of a person's skin

checking
blocking another player with one's body or hockey stick

competitive
having participants who want to be better than others at a sport or activity

energized
to have a lot of energy

ESPYs
a famous awards show presented by ESPN, a sports TV network

interviewed
to be asked questions

media
television, newspapers, magazines, radio, or other ways to communicate information to a large number of people

public image
how someone or something is seen by the world

stickhandling
using a hockey stick to control the puck

strain
when a part of the body is hurt from stretching it too far or overworking it

superstitious
to believe that unrelated actions or routines can affect the outcome of an event, such as a sports game

FURTHER
INFORMATION

Fishman, Jon M. *Hockey's G.O.A.T.: Wayne Gretzky, Sidney Crosby, and More*. Minneapolis: Lerner Publications, 2020.

Hockey Hall of Fame
https://www.hhof.com

Mikoley, Kate. *Hockey: Stats, Facts, and Figures*. New York: Gareth Stevens Publishing, 2018.

Nagelhout, Ryan. *Hockey: Who Does What?* New York: Gareth Stevens Publishing, 2018.

National Hockey League
https://www.nhl.com

Savage, Jeff. *Hockey Super Stats*. Minneapolis: Lerner Publications, 2018.

USA Hockey
https://www.usahockey.com

INDEX

ABOUT THE AUTHOR

James Monson is a sportswriter based in the Minneapolis-Saint Paul area. He has written articles that have appeared in various publications across the country. He has a degree in print/digital sports journalism.